THE GREAT ARTISTS
& THEIR WORLD
GAUGUIN

NEW
FOREST
PRESS

Publisher: Melissa Fairley
Editor: Guy Croton
Designer: Carol Davis
Production Controller: Ed Green
Production Manager: Suzy Kelly

ISBN: 978-1-84898-316-8
Library of Congress Control Number: 2010925211
Tracking number: nfp0004

North American edition copyright © TickTock Entertainment Ltd. 2010
First published in North America in 2010 by New Forest Press,
PO Box 784, Mankato, MN 56002
www.newforestpress.com

Printed in the USA
9 8 7 6 5 4 3 2 1

CONTENTS

INTRODUCTION

One of the most remarkable artists of the late nineteenth century, Paul Gauguin had a profound influence on the development of twentieth century art. Initially a stockbroker, in his late thirties he left his job and his wife and five children in order to pursue his artistic dreams.

DIFFERENT MOVEMENTS

As an artist, Gauguin struggled as he worked against popular opinion. He firstly became an Impressionist, but ended up classed as a Post-Impressionist with his flat, boldly colored style. Through experimenting with Symbolism, painting images of dreams, memories, and feelings, mixed with Cloisonnism, which described art that separated flat areas of color with black lines, he started a movement called Synthetism. His interest in Primitive art led to another movement called Primitivism. He also inspired Les Nabis, which means prophet in Hebrew and Arabic, which was a group of younger artists who followed some of his ideas.

Born in Paris in the middle of the nineteenth century, Gauguin traveled to Peru with his family when he was a baby. Tragically, his father died on the voyage, leaving Paul, his mother, and his sister to continue by themselves. They lived in Lima with his mother's family for four years. The colorful city and his comfortable life there later influenced Gauguin's art, but the family soon returned to France. Despite being interested in art, when Gauguin grew up, he conformed to his family's expectations and worked as a stockbroker for eleven years. He married a Danish girl, Mette, and over ten years, they had five children.

A year after his marriage, in 1874, Gauguin saw the first Impressionist exhibition in Paris and was captivated. He bought works by Manet, Monet, Sisley, Pissarro, Renoir, and Guillaumin and he began painting as a hobby. Encouraged by Pissarro, in 1876 one of his paintings was accepted at the Salon, the official annual art exhibition in Paris. Pissarro introduced him to Cézanne—an artist who was receiving a great deal of criticism from the art world and the public. Fascinated by Cézanne's revolutionary approach, Gauguin bought some of his paintings too. Gauguin exhibited with the Impressionists at four of their eight exhibitions. In 1882, there was a stock market crash. Gauguin lost his job and decided to work full-time as an artist. But after two years of struggling to make a living, he left Mette and the children with her family in Denmark. He went to Pont-Aven in Brittany to paint and live more cheaply. While the rest of France was becoming industrialized, the people of Pont-Aven lived simply, resisting modern ways. There, Gauguin moved away from Impressionism and developed his flat, colorful style, focusing on simplified lines and symbolism, expressing only the essence of a subject.

At the end of the nineteenth century, many young avant-garde artists wanted to overcome accepted traditions of art in order to portray new ways of looking at the world. They felt that the art of earlier cultures was more honest and natural than sophisticated academic art, where technical skill and classical ideas were imperative. Gauguin became one of the leading artists of this approach and spent his life trying to create a modern version of primitive art. He spent time in Panama and Martinique, searching for new ideas and methods and then he went to stay with van Gogh in the south of France. They planned to establish an artists' colony there, but the two artists had too many conflicting ideas and within weeks, they quarreled violently and Gauguin left. Disillusioned with France, he eventually moved to

Tahiti believing that he would find a simple, unspoiled way of life where he could create the art he dreamed of. Unfortunately, Tahiti had become quite modernized and was not as idyllic as he had hoped, but he studied the methods of local craftsmen and tried to make his own art more exotic, like the images he had seen in books about Polynesia. His work was appreciated by a few, but he spent the final years of his life poor, sick, and alone. Within three years of his death however, a large exhibition of his work was held in Paris and he was acknowledged as one of the greatest artists of his time.

Paul Gauguin and Mette Sofie Gad married in 1873 and settled quickly into family life. The first of their five children was born in 1874, and they moved to a large house in the Parisian suburbs. Until this time there is no record of Gauguin's interest in art. It may have been Gustave Arosa who first stimulated Gauguin's interest; Arosa owned a private collection of some importance with paintings by Delacroix, Courbet, and Corot as well as more "modern" pictures by the Impressionist Pissarro. Gauguin started buying paintings himself, concentrating on the new style with artists such as Monet, Renoir, Degas, and Cézanne. He also started painting, attending a few art classes and setting up a studio in his house. In 1876, Gauguin's painting of *Undergrowth at Viroflay* was accepted for exhibition at the Paris Salon. He took a less taxing job in order to have more time to paint. In 1883, after the financial disasters of the stock market crash, Gauguin gave up work to become a full-time painter.

BRETON GIRLS DANCING, 1888

Gauguin's wife, Mette, gave up hope of her husband supporting her and their five children as an artist. She returned to Denmark, supporting herself and the children by working as a French teacher. In 1885 the family were re-united as Gauguin tried a fresh start in Rouen. His paintings did not sell, however, and Mette eventually took the children back to Copenhagen with the exception of their third child, Clovis, who stayed with Paul. In 1886, he moved to Brittany, a popular (and inexpensive) summer destination for artists. Gauguin was to find the Brittany landscape and its inhabitants a rich source of imagery for his painting, to which he would return again and again.

THE WORLD OF GAUGUIN

Eugéne Henri Paul Gauguin (known as Paul) was born in Paris on the June 7, 1848. His father, Clovis Gauguin, was editor of the liberal newspaper *National*. His mother, Aline Marie Chazal, was just 22 years old when Paul was born and already had one daughter called Marie. Aline's mother was part Spanish, and had powerful and wealthy relatives in Peru. Gauguin's parents were encouraged to start a new life in Peru after Louis Napoleon Bonaparte's election to president of the French Republic in 1848. The newspaper *National*, under Clovis Gauguin's editorship, had been critical of Napoleon, and Clovis decided there was no future for the Gauguin family in France. So Paul Gauguin's early years were spent in Peru. When he was six years old he returned to France, and to boarding school in Orléans. His unhappy schooldays were filled with memories of happier times in Peru and as soon as he was old enough to leave he joined the merchant navy, embarking as officer-in-training on a ship bound for South America. Gauguin was to spend his whole life seeking the lost paradise of his childhood.

PHOTO OF LIMA IN THE 19TH CENTURY

Clovis and Aline Gauguin with their children Paul and Marie set sail for South America on August 8, 1849. Tragedy struck early when Clovis died of a heart attack en route, and was buried in Patagonia. Aline arrived with her two children at Lima to be met by her great-uncle, who held considerable political power and wealth. Consequently the Gauguins entered a paradise world with servants attending to their needs and no fear for their financial security. Their home was described as: *"a vast and luxurious residence where grand receptions were given and the most eminent figures of the Peruvian government mingled."* However a civil war forced the Gauguins to return to France in 1855.

AN OFFICER IN TRAINING

When Gauguin was 16, he entered the merchant navy, joining the ship *Luzitano* as officer-in-training, bound for Rio de Janeiro. While on an Atlantic crossing in 1867, his mother died. Aline had named a Parisian friend, Gustave Arosa, as legal guardian of the Gauguin children. After Paul had served his time in the French Navy on board the *Jérôme-Napoléon* (similar to the ship shown right) he returned to Paris in 1871, to live with his sister in the rue la Bruyere, near the Arosa family. Gustave Arosa arranged for Gauguin to take up a job as a stockbroker in the Paris stock exchange. Not long afterward he met a young Danish governess named Mette Gad, who he married in 1873.

INFLUENCES & EARLY WORKS

EFFECTS OF SNOW ON THE RUE CARCEL

This painting, made in 1883, shows Gauguin's work when he was under the influence of Pissarro and the Impressionist group. Pissarro himself made a number of snow scene paintings and Gauguin's painting of the fleeting effects of snow on the landscape are in line with the Impressionist's desire to capture the transitory nature of the landscape in its different conditions.

Gauguin had no real formal training as an artist and did not take up painting until he was about 25 years old. His wife, Mette, said she did not know Paul had any interest in painting when they first met. His legal guardian, Gustave Arosa, was an undoubted influence serving to open Gauguin's eyes to art. Camille Pissarro became an important early influence, encouraging Gauguin as he did other promising artists such as Vincent van Gogh. In 1879, at Pissarro's invitation, Gauguin exhibited with the Impressionists' fourth exhibition. By the early 1880s, Gauguin was exhibiting regularly with the Impressionists and became a collector of works by other Impressionist artists. Gauguin's new artistic friends included the Impressionist painters but also the café society intellectuals. Writers such as Stéphane Mallarmé and Arthur Rimbaud, the leading Symbolist poets, encouraged artists such as Odilon Redon, and Paul Gauguin to join the Symbolist movement.

PORTRAIT OF PISSARRO AND GAUGUIN *(left)*

Camille Pissarro, some years older than Gauguin, became Gauguin's friend and artistic mentor. Pissarro was extremely influential, encouraging Gauguin to adopt the Impressionist techniques and to seek out the type of subject matter that the Impressionist artists depicted. The development of Gauguin's work toward Symbolism caused Pissarro to criticize him, saying of his highly Symbolist representations of Breton women and other canvases,
"I reproach him for pinching this (style) from Japanese and Byzantine and other painters. I reproach him for not applying his synthesis to our modern, completely social anti-authoritarian and anti-mystical philosophy... This is a step backward."

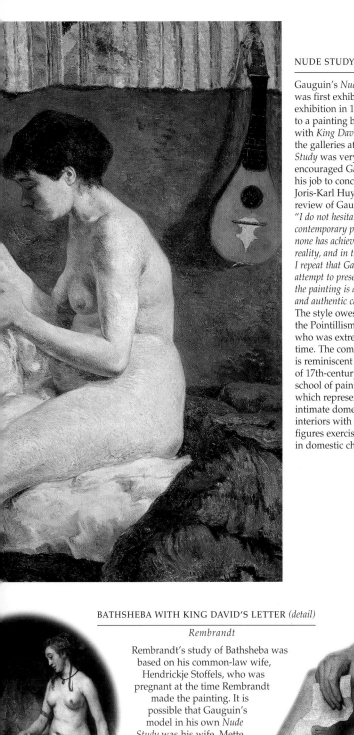

NUDE STUDY

Gauguin's *Nude Study*, painted in 1880, was first exhibited at the sixth Impressionist exhibition in 1881. It was immediately compared to a painting by Rembrandt entitled *Bathsheba with King David's Letter* which had entered the galleries at the Louvre in 1869. The *Nude Study* was very well received and no doubt encouraged Gauguin to consider giving up his job to concentrate on painting. The critic Joris-Karl Huysmans wrote a wholly favorable review of Gauguin's painting, stating: *"I do not hesitate to declare that, among the contemporary painters who have done nudes, none has achieved such a forceful note of reality, and in this I am not excepting Courbet... I repeat that Gauguin is the first in years to attempt to present a woman of our time... the painting is a complete success, a bold and authentic canvas."*
The style owes much to the Pointillism of fellow artist Georges Seurat, who was extremely influential at the time. The composition however is reminiscent of 17th-century Dutch school of painting, which represented intimate domestic interiors with figures exercised in domestic chores.

BATHSHEBA WITH KING DAVID'S LETTER *(detail)*

Rembrandt

Rembrandt's study of Bathsheba was based on his common-law wife, Hendrickje Stoffels, who was pregnant at the time Rembrandt made the painting. It is possible that Gauguin's model in his own *Nude Study* was his wife, Mette, who would have been pregnant at the time with their third child, Clovis.

THE ART OF HIS DAY

The conventions of 19th-century art were changed forever by the Realists, such as Courbet and Manet, who painted life as it truly was, depicting the peasants and prostitutes who inhabited the real world rather than idealized subjects or classical stories. Realism gave way to the Impressionists, who carried this notion even further, taking their paints and canvases outdoors, en plein air, in their attempt to capture the immediacy and spontaneity of life. Although Gauguin was heavily influenced by, and exhibited with, the Impressionists he started searching for a new style. By the mid-1880s, when Gauguin was trying to find his own way of painting, artists were completely freed from the belief that there was a "right way" to depict nature. It was suddenly understood that no objective view could exist; the passing of time, the changing light, the way in which the artist observed, all influenced the depiction of the subject. During the 1880s and 1890s, artists sought new ways of representing the world.

**THE YELLOW HOUSE
AT ARLES** (*detail*)

Vincent van Gogh

Another artist struggling to make his way at the same time as Gauguin was the Dutch-born painter Vincent van Gogh. The tragic story of this artist's life and death at his own hands is well known. Van Gogh was looking for a way of expressing himself through color. Many of his concerns about representing feelings through color and line were shared by Gauguin. The two lived together for a short period in 1888, when Gauguin went to stay with the lonely van Gogh at his little yellow house in Arles. The two quarreled, and to van Gogh's dismay, Gauguin left. Thrown into despair by his departure van Gogh severed his own ear.

NOTRE DAMES DES PORTES

Paul Serusier

Paul Gauguin developed a style of painting which was notable for the harsh black outlines around the subjects depicted and with flat areas of color within the lines, rather like stained glass. The style became known as Cloisonnism after the French word "*cloison*," meaning partition. He developed this way of painting while living in Pont-Aven in Brittany. Gauguin admitted a strong Japanese influence in his work which appeared increasingly graphic and abstract in nature. He led a small group of artists, known as the Pont-Aven School, who lived in the little village and were inspired by Gauguin. This included Paul Serusier as well as Charles Laval and Émile Bernard.

LA GRANDE JATTE

Georges Seurat

In 1886, Seurat's painting *La Grande Jatte* was shown at the eighth and last Impressionist exhibition in Paris. Seurat's painting was a sensation. The critics did not know what to make of this extraordinary painting executed in the "Pointillist" style, but it certainly was the center of attention. Seurat had for some time been working in a style that relied upon scientific principles relating to color theory. He painted with dots of color laid side-by-side, which when viewed from a distance blended together, "mixing" the colors in the viewer's eye, rather than on the canvas. Although the development of color photography and printing was in its infancy, Pointillism corresponded to the same scientific principles applied to the mechanical reproduction of images. Many artists experimented with this technique, including the Impressionist painter Pissarro and, in turn, Gauguin himself.

KITCHEN STILL LIFE *Paul Cézanne*

Cézanne took up painting after meeting Pissarro in Paris in 1861. He began to paint landscapes in the Impressionist style but his work developed away from Impressionist as he sought to *"make of Impressionism something solid and durable."* He advised artists to *"look for the cone, the sphere, and the cylinder in nature,"* and his work has been recognized as the foundation from which the Cubist style was built by Picasso and Braque at the beginning of the 20th century. Gauguin was a great admirer of Cézanne's work, making paintings that are clearly derivative of Cézanne's style. Gauguin purchased a Cézanne still-life which he called *"an exceptional pearl... I will only part with it when my last shirt is gone."*

THE LIFE OF GAUGUIN

~1848~
Paul Gauguin is born on June 7 as Eugéne Henri Paul Gauguin

~1849~
Gauguin and family sail for Peru—Gauguin's father, Clovis, dies en route

Gauguin lives in Lima with mother, Aline and sister, Marie

~1853~
Family return to Orléans, France

~1865~
Gauguin joins the merchant navy

~1867~
Gauguin's mother, Aline, dies while Gauguin is at sea

~1872~
Starts work as a stockbroker, paints as a hobby

~1873~
Marries Mette Gad

~1874~
Birth of their first child, Émile

~1877~
Birth of daughter, Aline

~1879~
Exhibits at the Impressionist exhibition

~1881~
Exhibits at sixth Impressionist exhibition, dealer Durand-Ruel buys paintings

Birth of Jean-René

~1883~
Loses job as a stockbroker and concentrates on painting

Birth of Paul

YOUNG GIRL ASLEEP

Gauguin's favorite child was Aline, the couple's second, born on December 24, 1877. She had been named after Gauguin's mother. Gauguin carried a photograph of his daughter with him when he left the family to go and live in Tahiti. He doubtless felt terrible guilt and sorrow when in 1897 he received a letter from Mette, informing him that Aline had died of pneumonia on January 19. Soon afterward, Gauguin took a dose of arsenic in a bid to kill himself, but recovered.

BUST OF METTE GAUGUIN *Jules-Ernest Bouillot*

Gauguin met Mette Gad in Paris, and they married in 1873, quickly settling into an uneventful routine in suburban Paris. Mette gave birth to the first of their five children in 1874. After Gauguin had devoted himself entirely to painting and steadily spent all their money, Mette had no alternative other than to return to her family in Denmark with the children. They were never to be properly re-united again. Gauguin wrote to Mette: *"there are two natures in me, the Indian and the sensitive man. The sensitive man has now disappeared, letting the Indian go ahead strong and straight."* After his travels to Brittany and Martinique, Gauguin finally set sail for Tahiti and said goodbye forever to his wife and children.

CAFÉ AT ARLES, 1888

Gauguin painted this picture when Vincent van Gogh's brother, Theo, arranged for Gauguin to go and stay with Vincent in Arles, in 1888. It was because Gauguin relied on art dealer Theo's financial support that he agreed rather than out of a desire to stay with Vincent. Theo was anxious to provide support and friendship for his brother and Vincent's spirits were lifted at the news of Gauguin's agreement. He decorated Gauguin's room with paintings of sunflowers and thought of starting an artist's colony in Arles.

FAMILY, FRIENDS, & OTHERS

Gauguin's family background makes colorful reading. He undoubtedly had Spanish ancestors with Peruvian ties, but his claim that he was descended from Inca kings appears far-fetched. The most famous of his family was his maternal grandmother,

Gauguin with his eldest children— Émile and Aline.

Flora Tristan, who made a name for herself as a writer and dedicated feminist, advocating trade unions in the 1840s. Flora was the illegitimate daughter of Don Moscoso, whose family owned a large estate in Peru. Flora's unfaithful husband was jailed for 29 years after attempting to kill his wife. Their daughter, Aline, met and married Clovis Gauguin, whose political views earned him persecution from the State, and prompted the Gauguin family to move to Peru to seek the support of Don Moscoso.

THE FAMILY SCHUFFENECKER, 1889

When Gauguin returned from his travels to Martinique he first went back to Brittany, then in 1889 to Paris, where he stayed with Émile Schuffenecker and his family. Schuffenecker was a fellow painter with whom Gauguin had worked in his days as a stockbroker in the 1870s, at Banque Bertin. His portrait of the family is not a complimentary one. Émile is unsympathetically depicted, almost caricature-like, standing in the background looking towards his seated wife and children. Madame Schuffenecker, whom Gauguin had tried to seduce, leading to bad feeling between the two men, is shown with a claw-like hand. Despite Schuffenecker's help and financial support, the picture dismisses Émile's work as an artist by turning his canvas side-on so it is invisible to the viewer.

PAYSAGE DE MARTINIQUE, 1887

This view of the landscape of Saint Pierre bay deliberately depicts a tropical paradise untouched by an outside hand. In reality it was a developed town with European architecture (including a church with a steeple) and a busy port.

Gauguin's technique, breaking up the trees into blocks of color, is reminiscent of Cézanne's approach to landscape, which was so influential at the time. Nevertheless, Gauguin is beginning to demonstrate a confident style of his own and one notable art critic commented on Gauguin's Martinique paintings: *"He has finally conquered his own personality... he is his own master."*

Although Gauguin made no more than a dozen paintings in Martinique and returned after just a few months abroad, the experience was very important for him. He had discovered the tropical light and color that made his paintings come alive, and had glimpsed his own "paradise world" that he sought to recapture.

A contemporary description of Martinique likens the island to *"one of the most precious pearls of France's colonial jewel box."* It should be remembered that the relationship between the artist and the place was one determined very much by France's dominion over its colonial outpost. Despite Gauguin's poverty, his observations of the landscape and people reflect his own French (and Parisian) culture which tended to idealize the exotic, "primitive" land and inhabitants. Gauguin's Western eye sought not only the secure, carefree existence of his early childhood, but the supposed simplicity of an "undeveloped" society uncorrupted by Western values. When subsequently shown in Paris, Gauguin's paintings of Martinique were described as *"divine, Eden-like."*

WANDERLUST

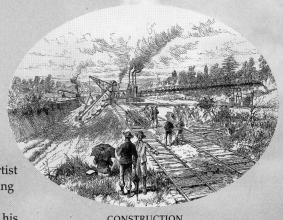

CONSTRUCTION
OF THE PANAMA CANAL

Gauguin's first attempt to recapture the happy and exotic memories of his lost youth in South America came in 1887, when he decided to journey to Panama with fellow artist Charles Laval. Gauguin was desperate to bring about a change in his life; he was hopelessly hard up, unable to bring in any money from his painting, and described Paris as "a wilderness for a poor man." The idea was to seek the support of Gauguin's brother-in-law who lived in Panama. Before they set off, Mette visited Gauguin to collect their son, Clovis, who had been living with him, and returned to Denmark with Clovis and a number of Gauguin's paintings. Laval and Gauguin set sail on April 10, 1887 but stayed only a short time in Panama, before moving on to the Caribbean island of Martinique.

Gauguin's money ran out soon after arriving in Panama. His brother-in-law provided no help and Gauguin got a job along with hundreds of others who had traveled to Panama to work for the Panama Canal Construction Company. In the 1880s, a railway ran across the strip of land linking the Atlantic and Pacific Oceans but ships had to sail thousands of miles around South America. The attempt to build a canal linking the two oceans failed when the company went bankrupt, and it was not until 1914 that the Panama canal was finally opened.

SAINT PIERRE, MARTINIQUE

Work for the Panama Canal Construction Company did not last long. Gauguin was laid off after 15 days and the two friends went to Saint Pierre on the island of Martinique. Both Laval and Gauguin were seriously ill, having picked up malaria and dysentery, diseases which spread rapidly among the workforce in the swampy conditions in Panama. Some years after Gauguin's visit, the town of Saint Pierre was destroyed by a volcanic eruption that killed most of the 30,000 population. Today, it is a thriving holiday destination.

SYMBOLISM

The Symbolist writer Albert Aurier chose The Vision after the Sermon to write about his theories in an article entitled Symbolism in painting: Gauguin. He writes: *"Far, far away on a fabulous hill, whose soil appears as a gleaming vermilion, we see the biblical struggle between Jacob and the Angel. While these two legendary giants.... fight their formidable battle, some naive, interested women observe them...They have the respectful poses of simple creatures listening to extraordinary tales... they are in a church... and the venerated voice of the old priest hovers over their heads... All these surrounding objects have dissipated into the vapors; even the storyteller himself has disappeared, leaving only his voice... and it is that voice, that provincially fantastic vision that rises up over there, far, far away..."*

THE VISION AFTER THE SERMON, 1888

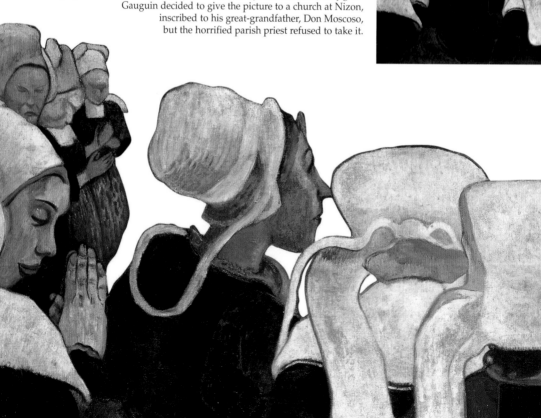

This painting was a turning point in Gauguin's career as a painter. The themes of Breton women and wrestling angels are expressed in a spiritual way, far removed from the Impressionist adherence to the depiction of the real and everyday world around them. Stylistically Gauguin breaks ground with his contemporaries, adopting a technique which is almost poster-like in its graphic approach. Gauguin described it as: *"a religious painting...There are Breton women praying, their costumes a deep black... the two bonnets on the right are like monstrous helmets—dark purple apple tree stretches across the canvas... the ground is pure vermilion... the angel is dressed in ultramarine-violet, and Jacob is bottle green. The angel's wings are pure chrome... For me the landscape and the fight in this picture exist only in the imagination of the people praying after the sermon, that is why there is a contrast between the naturalness of the people and the unnatural, disproportionate landscape that surrounds the fight."* Gauguin decided to give the picture to a church at Nizon, inscribed to his great-grandfather, Don Moscoso, but the horrified parish priest refused to take it.

FAMOUS IMAGES

Gauguin returned to Brittany in 1888, but his thoughts were never far from Martinique. He experimented with new ways of painting, creating compositions which represented a new way of seeing things. The experience of painting in the tropics influenced his Breton paintings, which broke the last ties he had with the Impressionist style. His work now included flat fields of color, not graduated or containing nuances of tone. The shapes of figures and objects were clearly separated with black lines in a way reminiscent of stained glass painting and also of Japanese graphic art. The traditional techniques of color variations and perspectives were abandoned, but instead of following the Impressionist view of the world, Gauguin now sought to depict his own inner view. His paintings began to deal with imaginary and symbolic subject matter whose meaning was not immediately apparent to the viewer.

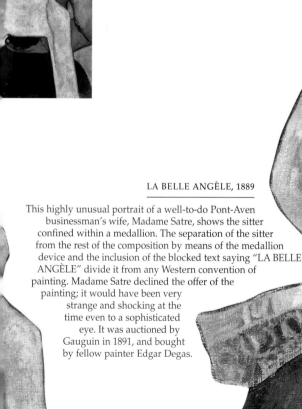

LA BELLE ANGÈLE, 1889

This highly unusual portrait of a well-to-do Pont-Aven businessman's wife, Madame Satre, shows the sitter confined within a medallion. The separation of the sitter from the rest of the composition by means of the medallion device and the inclusion of the blocked text saying "LA BELLE ANGÈLE" divide it from any Western convention of painting. Madame Satre declined the offer of the painting; it would have been very strange and shocking at the time even to a sophisticated eye. It was auctioned by Gauguin in 1891, and bought by fellow painter Edgar Degas.

THE MARTYR

The Universal Exhibition was held in 1889 at the Palais des Beaux-Arts in Paris, celebrating the centenary of the French Revolution. It included an "official" art exhibition which refused to include avant-garde artists such as the Impressionists. An independent exhibition was organized by Émile Schuffenecker at the Café des Arts, to show works by "refused"

STILL LIFE WITH JAPANESE PRINT, 1889

The independent exhibition attracted criticism and scorn from many, which stung Gauguin and he decided to return to Brittany. However Albert Aurier wrote: *"A small section is lacking in the Palais des Beaux-Arts for the few independent artists who, unknown to or scorned by the public... are working far from the official schools and academies, researching and developing a new kind of art, that will, perhaps, be the art of tomorrow."*

artists immediately next to the official exhibition area. The title of the independent exhibition was *Impressionniste et Synthétiste*, which clearly signaled the difference between the paintings of the Impressionists and the Synthetists such as Gauguin, Émile Bernard, and Charles Laval. The show did not make money but did create a stir among the contemporary art scene. The Synthetist painters intended to express their ideas and emotions through the use of brilliant colors which could also be used decoratively. They rejected any naturalistic representation of their subject in favor of creating a pictorial "synthesis"; an essence of the idea which inspired the picture. However, the Universal Exhibition with its exhibits from distant parts of the French colonial empire spurred Gauguin to think again about leaving for the tropics once more.

CHRIST IN THE GARDEN OF OLIVES, 1889

Gauguin was discouraged by the criticism of his work and felt alone. In this self-portrait as Christ in the Garden of Olives he places himself clearly in the role of the forsaken Christ awaiting betrayal. This identification demonstrates how much he felt the rejection of his art, how apparently hopeless was the quest for success and that his martyrdom was inevitable. He explained the picture by stating: *"It represents the crushing of an ideal, and a pain that is both divine and human. Jesus is totally abandoned, his disciples are leaving him..."* Gauguin was soon to decide that he should cut himself off from friends and critics alike: *"I am leaving for Tahiti, and I hope to stay there for the rest of my days. I think that my work...is but a seed that I can cultivate there in that wild and primitive place. For that I must have peace. What does it matter that the glory will belong to others?"*

SELF-PORTRAIT IN FRONT OF THE YELLOW CHRIST, 1889

Gauguin's paintings made while he was in Brittany included many representations of religious subjects. His imagery, depicted in a primitive style, showed the devout Breton peasants, the suffering Christ, and the Pietà. Although Gauguin was not particularly religious, he sympathized with the devotion of the Breton people and sought to capture the sense of passion and emotion. He portrayed himself in front of one of his own paintings, the *Yellow Christ*, thereby immediately identifying with the figure of Christ. His model for the crucifixion was a statue in the chapel of Tremalo, near the town of Pont-Aven. The expression on Gauguin's face is grave, and his gaze is serious and intent, full of resolve.

AREAREA, 1892

The title of this painting has been translated as "amusement" or "happiness" depending upon which interpretation of the Tahitian word is taken. The scene is possibly set at evening time; two seated female figures sit under a tree while three others stand in the distance next to a statue of Hina, Tahitian goddess of the moon. One of the women plays a flute while the other, dressed in a white robe, stares boldly at the viewer. The foreground is dominated by an orange dog whose color and presence in the picture has been suggested by some critics to represent evil. This is one of Gauguin's most successful Tahitian pictures painted after he had been on the island for a year. Its carefully controlled use of color and composition create a harmonious effect while the dog and staring woman maintain a sense of mystery, even menace.

WOMAN WITH A FLOWER, 1891

Gauguin arrived at Papeete, capital of Tahiti, on June 9, 1891. He was disappointed to find that European culture had already left its mark on the town and that the inhabitants had turned their backs on their own culture; a small but influential French community dominated Papeete. Gauguin decided to leave for a remote area of Tahiti where the European influence was not so profound. The truth of the matter, however, was that Gauguin was 50 years too late. The Tahitian society he looked for had been changed beyond recognition by decades of rule by white European colonialists. In this portrait, with the Tahitian name of *Vahine Note Tiare*, he shows a Tahitian woman wearing a European-style dress approved by the missionaries.

20

THE ARTIST'S VISION
ESCAPE

By 1889 Gauguin had decided to leave France for the tropics in the hope of finding a simpler, cheaper place to live and work, dissatisfied with the Brittany villages crowded with artists and from where he could still *"hear the jeers of Paris."* He was not discouraged by his earlier trip to Martinique, and still believed he could find the exotic, happy, and secure place of his early childhood. In April 1889, he wrote: *"I have decided to leave for Madagascar... Madame Redon says that with 5,000 francs you can live there for 30 years if you want to."* However, he began to receive conflicting advice about the cost of living in Madagascar and other destinations under consideration such as Tonkin (now known as Vietnam). Eventually, Gauguin decided on Tahiti because Madagascar was *"too near the civilized world."* Gauguin auctioned 30 paintings to raise money for the voyage and all but one sold. The total sales made 7,350 francs. He traveled to Copenhagen to say farewell to his wife and family, after which he headed for Marseilles. On April 1, 1891 he embarked upon the ship *Océanien*, for Tahiti.

VIRGIN WITH CHILD, 1891

The Tahitian title *Ia Orana Maria*, inscribed in the box at the bottom of the painting, translates as "We greet thee, Mary," the Angel Gabriel's words to the Virgin Mary. In the foreground stands the figure of Mary, a Tahitian woman with a child upon her shoulders. Both woman and child have haloes encircling their heads. The Angel Gabriel can be seen in the background on the left, partially obscured by trees. Gauguin's painting of a Christian subject is depicted in a style which borrows heavily from traditional European painting. The costumes and exotic fruits in the foreground, however, remove the painting from this European context and the two female figures facing Mary, stand in the Buddhist prayer pose. The painting can be seen as a representation of the conflicting religious influences at the time.

WHAT, ARE YOU JEALOUS?, 1892

The composition of this painting
entitled *Aha oe feii* is similar to *Nafea faa
ipoipo* and *Women on the Beach*, but
what is striking about this painting is
the boldness with which the naked
women are portrayed. No longer are
his subjects dressed in the modest
missionary-approved long dresses or
even the local colorful wraps. The
seated figure appears to be posing the
question to the viewer rather than to
the figure lying on the beach, an
impression reinforced by the woman's
sideways glance at the viewer.

WHAT DO THE PAINTINGS SAY?

Gauguin was disappointed with his surroundings
in Papeete, the Tahitian capital. It was a busy town,
with as many Europeans and Chinese tradesmen as
Tahitians. Gauguin was anxious to paint subjects
which represented the traditional Tahitian way of
life, its customs, culture, and religion. He found
little opportunity to do so in Papeete, so he moved
to Mataiea which was some 30 miles (50 km)
distant, but the real Tahitian world continued
to elude him. Not only had European culture
changed forever the way in which the indigenous
population lived, but Gauguin deluded himself
when he thought that he had found a corner of the
world untouched by Western hands. He was so
keen to recreate the tropical paradise of his
childhood, that he pretended his paintings were
giving a first-hand insight into a disappearing
culture. In fact Gauguin's images were heavily
influenced by a book of Tahitian customs which
had been given to him by a colonist living in Tahiti.
Nevertheless Gauguin's pictures became the true
image of Tahitian life in the eyes of the Western
world and remain so today, reinforced by
Hollywood film clichés depicting unspoilt
Tahitian islands, beautiful
women, and food which
falls from the trees.

WOMEN OF ALGIERS *(detail)*

Eugéne Delacroix

Gauguin took many prints with him to Tahiti. He referred
freely to these reproductions of paintings by well-known artists
and in many cases used the motifs in his own work. This detail
from Delacroix's *Women of Algiers* compares to the seated
figures in several of Gauguin's Tahitian paintings. Gauguin
deliberately transposed Western subjects, painting them in
a Tahitian setting, attempting to place his own work in the
context of the European art that he admired.

WHEN WILL YOU MARRY?, 1892 (NAFEA FAA IPOIPO)

The question in the title of this painting is probably being posed by the woman in the background to the woman whose wish to find a husband is expressed according to Tahitian ritual—a flower worn behind her ear. Gauguin priced this picture at 1,500 francs when it finally went on show in Paris, higher than any other canvas. Gauguin's work appealed to a Parisian audience fascinated by the exoticism of far-away Pacific islands. The subject may even have been deliberately chosen to illustrate a theme with which a French audience would have been familiar because of the popularity of the book, *Le Mariage de Loti*, written by Julien Viaud in 1880. This book, which portrayed Tahiti as an exotic paradise, captured the imagination of its European readers. Viaud had visited Tahiti as a young naval officer and had a relationship with a Tahitian. He was given the Tahitian name Loti, the name of a kind of flower.

TWO TAHITIAN WOMEN ON THE BEACH, 1891

This picture portrays the activity of collecting the vegetal fibers that were to be found on the beach and which the Tahitian women used for weaving. Strands of the fiber can be seen in the hands of the woman wearing the pink dress. The fibers are coiled into a stylized pattern. Gauguin painted an almost identical picture entitled *Parau Api—Women on the Beach*, which translates as *What News?*

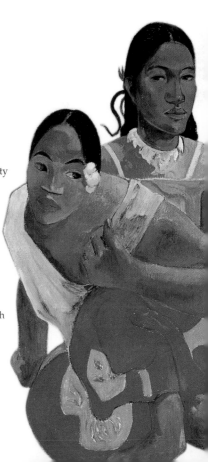

**TAHITIAN
WOODEN FIGURE**

Gauguin made many references
to Tahitian idols, both in his
paintings and sculptures. These
were often imaginary figures
based partly on Tahitian idols,
but also freely adapted from
Easter Island statues and other
stone sculptures found in the
area. His recreation of *Oviri moe-
ahere*, the goddess of death,
appears in paintings and
sculptures and had a special
significance for Gauguin who
asked for a version to be on
his gravestone. His wish was
finally granted in 1973.

WHAT DO THE
PAINTINGS SAY?

These words, written in Gauguin's
notebook, echoed those of Delacroix;
*"...there is an impression that results from
a certain arrangement of colors, of light, of
shadows. One might call it the music of
painting. Even before you know anything
about a painting, you enter a cathedral and
you find yourself too far from the picture to
know what it represents, yet often you are
struck by this magical harmony. Herein
lies painting's true superiority over other
arts, for this emotion addresses the most
intimate part of the soul."* Gauguin
was never far from Western
traditions in the stylistic execution of
his subject matter, as this reference to
Delacroix shows, and even his subjects
reflect the overlaying of Western cultural
influences over indigenous Tahitian
culture. This is most evident in the
continuing religious references in the
paintings, where European imagery sits
alongside Polynesian imagery. In fact,
years of colonial rule had eroded much
of the local way of life, and Gauguin
sought to resurrect local customs in
his paintings which had long-since
been forgotten.

OLYMPIA (detail)
by Édouard Manet

THE SPIRIT & THE GHOST

Spirit of the Dead Watching shows the young girl *Teha'amana* lying
on her bed, in fear of the tupapaus—the spirits of the dead. The
Tahitians believed that sleeping in the dark made them vulnerable
to these spirits which often appeared in the form of phosphoresences.
Gauguin shows the spirits as flowers in the background. He describes
painting them: *"like sparks of light,"* and goes on to say: *"I made the ghost
quite simply like a little old lady; because the girl, not knowing French theatrical
images of spirits, can only imagine... a human being like herself."*

NEVERMORE, 1897

Gauguin described this painting in a letter to a friend: *"With a simple nude I wished to suggest a certain long-gone barbaric luxury. It is all drowned in colors which are deliberately somber...its title, 'Nevermore' not exactly the raven from Edgar Poe, but the bird of the devil which keeps watch."* Again there is a reference to Manet, both through *Olympia* and his illustrations of Edgar Allen Poe's poem *The Raven*.

SPIRIT OF THE DEAD WATCHING, 1892 (MANAO TUPAPAU)

This powerful painting (below) demonstrates the varying influences which make up Gauguin's painting. There is a clear reference to Édouard Manet's painting *Olympia*, which had caused a storm when first exhibited in Paris in 1865, and which had itself looked back to earlier paintings by Titian and Goya. Gauguin had made a copy of Manet's painting and knew it well. *Manao Tupapau* also contained references to Tahitian folklore, not appreciated by Gauguin at first hand, as he would like his audience to think, but from J. A. Moerenhout's book *Voyages aux Îles de Grand Océan*, first published in 1837 and read by Gauguin in 1892. This influential book charted the customs and rituals of Polynesia before they had been eroded by European colonialism.

CLAY JUG IN THE FORM OF A SEVERED HEAD

Gauguin made several "stoneware" clay pots. This was a type of pottery defined by the clay used and how it was fired. This one was made in response to witnessing a public execution in Paris but shows Gauguin's own features. The gory red glazed finish appears as dripping blood.

MANAO TUPAPAU

Gauguin made a number of prints from woodcuts. The surface of a panel of wood was carved to produce an image "in reverse." The parts of the surface left untouched were rolled with ink or paint so that when pressed onto paper these parts left a "positive" image behind. The parts of the wood carved away did not carry any ink so they appeared as light areas on the paper. Gauguin then colored many of these woodcut prints with watercolor so each print was different.

BE MYSTERIOUS

Gauguin carved this lime wood panel in 1890. It is a companion piece to a panel carved a year earlier entitled *Be in love and you will be happy*. Gauguin was very pleased with his carved panel and valued it at three times the price of his paintings. The imagery looks very exotic but it was made before he traveled to Tahiti. The modeling to the back of the central figure is very accomplished and it may be that Gauguin first practiced wood carving while on his long sea voyages both as sailor and passenger. Carving in wood and other materials was a common craft among sailors who often had long periods of time to spare, and invariably both a knife and pieces of wood to hand.

HOW WERE THEY MADE?

Gauguin experimented with many different types of materials and ways of creating images. He had no real formal training although he had help from the likes of Pissarro early in his painting career. He was happy to experiment with wood carving and clay modeling as well as oil painting, and developed a great love of wood carving when in Tahiti. He

occasionally tried his hand at watercolors and less conventional means of producing pictures such as woodcut prints. In order to explain his experiences in Tahiti he decided to make a book which carried the title *Noa Noa*, which might be translated as "rich in fragrances." The book, written in Gauguin's own hand complete with corrections, was highly illustrated. He made a series of woodcut prints in a deliberately "primitive" style with decorative borders and hand painted in water-color. These prints were for *Noa Noa* but also to be sold as printed images. Gauguin had problems getting supplies of paint when he was in Tahiti. To add to his problems he found that the climate made the paint dry very quickly so he had to adjust his way of painting accordingly. He ordered Lefranc's decorators' colors from France because they were inexpensive.

OVIRI MOE-AHERE

This highly unusual sculpture of *Oviri moe-ahere*, the "savage" goddess of death who is also known as murderess *La Tueuse*, is modeled in clay. The figure holds a wolf cub while a dead wolf lies under her feet. Gauguin made the figure on his return to Paris from Tahiti in 1894. It was made at Ernest Chaplet's studio from clay, modeled like a vase, creating a hollow center. Gauguin submitted the sculpture to Beaux-Arts Salon which refused it. An indignant Gauguin wrote to the newspaper *Le Soir:* "*I had seen the possibility of giving a new thrust to ceramic art by creating new, handmade forms...to replace the (potter's) wheel with intelligent hands that could communicate to the vase the life of a figure while remaining faithful to the character of the material...this was my aim.*" After his death a bronze cast of the figure was eventually made and stood at Gauguin's grave, as he had wished.

PHOTO OF TOHOTAUA

Tohotaua was an exceptionally beautiful young Marquesan who was a model for several paintings including *Young girl with a Fan and Contes barbares* (see page 32). Tohotaua is thought by some to be the wife of Haapuani, a local magician and friend of Gauguin's. The photograph was taken in Gauguin's house and in the background it is possible to see reproductions hanging on the wall. The painting of *Mrs Holbein and Her Children* can be identified, as can *Dancers and Harlequin* by Edgar Degas and *Hope* by Pierre Puvis de Chavannes. This is clear evidence of the continued interest Gauguin demonstrated in the artistic works of others, and it is known that he carried with him to Tahiti many reproductions of paintings. The fact that Gauguin copied some of his compositions directly from those reproductions shows that he not only maintained an interest in traditional European art but did not fear showing that interest.

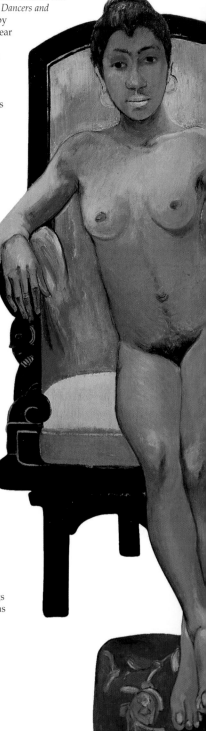

ANNAH THE JAVANESE

Gauguin painted this portrait of Annah, who was in fact part Sri Lankan (then Ceylon) and part Malay, when he was in France in 1894. He had become infatuated with the 13-year-old girl much to the disgust of his family who were still in touch with Gauguin from their home in Denmark. To make matters worse he added a title in Tahitian which is just about visible on the top right of the picture. This reads *Aita tamari vahine Judith te parari* which can be translated as "The child woman Judith is not yet breached." It does not refer to Annah at all but to another young acquaintance, the 12-year-old Judith Erikson-Molard.

MRS HOLBEIN
& HER CHILDREN

Hans Holbein the Younger

This was one of the many paintings by different artists whose work was carried with Gauguin to Tahiti in reproduction form.

A VIEW OF WOMEN

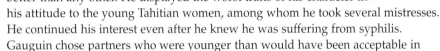

Gauguin was attracted to the way of life in Tahiti which he saw as a
"primitive splendor" without the material concerns of his native France.
He had hoped to be able to live simply, to paint without the need to do
any other work to earn his living, and to be free from the petty
politics of critics and artists alike. However, when he returned to
Tahiti for the last time in 1895 he was lonely, plagued by ill-health
and unable to change the fact that he, too, was an outsider in this
society; another French colonial whose behavior was sometimes no
better than any other. He displayed the worst traits of his character in
his attitude to the young Tahitian women, among whom he took several mistresses.
He continued his interest even after he knew he was suffering from syphilis.
Gauguin chose partners who were younger than would have been acceptable in
European society. These mistresses were the models for a number of paintings,
often as anonymous models but sometimes sitting for portraits under their
own names. Gauguin's bohemian lifestyle was unacceptable at home and
became problematic in Tahiti when he upset the local community.

YOUNG GIRL WITH FAN, 1902

Tohotaua was the model for this painting which is clearly based on
the photograph taken by Gauguin. The artist makes some key
changes to the photograph, however, by making her gaze into
space instead of engaging the viewer's eye directly, and
removing the pareo, or wrap. Tohotaua holds a fan in
front of her, partially covering her nakedness. This
portrait is an image of a Polynesian woman which is
entirely of Gauguin's making, but which has now
become a standard representation of the
women of the South Sea Islands.

THE UNANSWERED QUESTIONS

ALINE
GAUGUIN
c.1895
———

Gauguin returned to Tahiti in 1895. He built a house at Punaania, just south of Papeete, where he lived with Pahura, his new mistress. Things quickly went wrong and his health and finances failed him. In 1896, a daughter was born to Gauguin and his *vahine* (mistress), but the baby died shortly after birth. In April 1897, he received a letter from his wife, Mette, informing him that their daughter Aline had died of pneumonia. Gauguin was plunged into deep depression by the news of Aline's death and finally attempted suicide by taking an overdose of arsenic. He recovered to have two more children, but syphilis claimed his life six years later.

WHERE DO WE COME FROM? WHAT ARE WE? WHERE ARE WE GOING?, 1897

"I wanted, before dying, to paint a large picture that preoccupied me during that whole month; I worked day and night in an extraordinary fever." Gauguin painted a monumental work, the biggest he ever painted, and called it *Where do we come from? What are we? Where are we going?* It is regarded by many as his last important picture. After finishing his painting he walked to the top of a nearby hill and took a massive

The old woman represents the end of life.

This is not a Tahitian goddess but represents a woman becoming an idol.

The scene is compared with the Garden of Eden. This figure appears to be taking a fruit from the tree of knowledge.

The white bird with the lizard in its claws, represents the futility of vain words.

The painting is an inventory of the world, and includes people, animals, vegetation, rocks, water, and sky.

The child represents the beginning of life.

dose of arsenic; however, he took so much he simply made himself sick. He never managed to paint anything to equal this huge painting in the final six years of his life. The painting was made on a 13 ft (4 m) length of sackcloth material, and was probably prepared from drawings made on squared-up tracing paper despite Gauguin's assertion that he made no preparations for the great work. Gauguin regarded Where do we come from? as a "philosophical work." He said it should be "read" from right to left: this way of reading is common with Eastern texts.

CONTES BARBARES, 1902

In this painting, the title of which can be translated as *Primitive Tales,* Gauguin presents three figures in a flower-filled landscape. It is difficult to tell whether the central figure sitting in the lotus position is male or female. On the right is a kneeling red-haired woman. On the left an extraordinary figure whose features are reminiscent of Meyer de Haan, Gauguin's friend from Pont-Aven in France. This man-creature has clawed feet like an animal and feline eyes. The writer Bengt Danielsson suggests that the red-haired woman who also appears in earlier paintings by Gauguin, is Tohotaua, wife of the sorcerer Haapuani. There is a coming together in this painting of Western thought, as represented by de Haan who was an occultist; Buddhism as represented by the central figure; and Maori folklore represented by the flame-haired wife of the Marquesan sorcerer. This combination would have appealed to the Symbolist Gauguin.

WHAT THE CRITICS SAY

Gauguin has been portrayed over the years as a defender of the Tahitian people against the corruption and insensitivity of the colonial Europeans. Certainly Gauguin likes to give this impression in his own writings, such as in his book, Noa Noa, where he describes his quarrels with the authorities. Gauguin's defense of the islanders, however, was as much to do with his own disagreement with these European powers as it was to do with sympathy for the local population. His attitudes were sometimes as bad as any colonialists. While Gauguin struggled to paint in his poverty-stricken state in Polynesia, his reputation as an artist began to grow in Europe. The critic Achille Delaroche wrote of: "the riches of this tropical vegetation, where an Edenic and free existence idles beneath lucky stars." This was the same Eden sought by Gauguin since his childhood.

RIDERS ON THE BEACH, 1902

Degas' work *Racehorses at Longchamps*, painted 27 years earlier, has been clearly identified by art historians as an influence on this late painting by Gauguin, of bareback riders on the beach. Gauguin was quite open about his debt to other artists and especially Degas, for whom he had tremendous admiration.The art historians and critics were slow to accept Gauguin into the world of Western art. The French art historian André Michel wrote a history of the acceptance of Gauguin's work which itself reveals how difficult it was for the art establishment to embrace wayward artists (Michel described van Gogh as "foreign and crazy"). Gradually, Michel and others came to appreciate and then applaud Gauguin's work and recognize his influence on others.

RACEHORSES AT
LONGCHAMPS *(detail)*

Edgar Degas

Gauguin's painting appears clumsy by comparison to Degas' masterly draughtsmanship, but Gauguin's work is both magical and sinister as the riders recede towards the horizon over a beach of pink sand. The composition would have been carefully constructed, as revealed in this extract from Gauguin's writings about another Degas picture: *"Before me is a photograph of a painting by Degas. The lines on the floor lead to a point on the horizon, very far, very high, intersected by dancers... What is the symbol? Is it eternal love... nothing like it... it is choreography."*

A LASTING IMPRESSION

By 1899 Gauguin's work was beginning to attract collectors. The dealer Ambroise Vollard struck an exclusive deal with Gauguin which was worth 250 francs per painting, and payments of 350 francs per month, to secure Gauguin's agreed output of 25 paintings per year. The income kept Gauguin going in his final years, although he occasionally needed to supplement this income from minor jobs he could get on the island. Gauguin died on May 8, 1903 at the age of 54. His work had begun to attract interest which accelerated after his death, although acceptance as a great artist came much later. Artists such as Odilon Redon, and Henri Rousseau were aware of Gauguin's images of lush vegetation when they painted their own visions of the tropics and the jungle. Gauguin's Synthetism, which accentuated color as a means of expressing ideas, became very important to the painters who followed, such as Pierre Bonnard, and Maurice Denis. Great artists such as Matisse and Picasso who were to dominate the early 20th century owed a debt to Gauguin's freedom with color. Later still, Gauguin's languid, dreamlike Polynesian landscapes became an often-quoted visual example of escape from the realities of life in the Western world.

SELLING AN IDEAL

Advertisers use the image of the "primitive" in the same way that Gauguin used images of Polynesia. The unspoilt Eden of the South Seas together with the promise of a way of life unrestricted by Western morals, is used time and again to sell products.

MUSEUM OF MODERN ART

Retrospective exhibitions of Gauguin's work began in earnest after his death. In October 1903, the year of his death, a retrospective including nine works was held at the Petit Palais in Paris. By 1907 a retrospective including 227 works was staged at the Grand Palais. When the Museum of Modern Art opened in New York in 1929 its collection included 21 works by Gauguin.

ART NOUVEAU

Gauguin's legacy of Symbolism was profound. Maurice Denis recalled being introduced to Gauguin's work in 1888. Eventually the influence spread to a small group who called themselves "prophets" (Nabis). Members of the Parisian group including Bonnard, Vuillard, and Denis were eager to acquaint themselves with more and more of Gauguin's work. Denis wrote in 1903: *"We understood thanks to Gauguin that every work of art is a transposition, a caricature, the impassioned equivalent of a felt sensation."* The influence also spread to the growing Art Nouveau movement, and it is possible to see clear links between Gauguin's cloisonné style, in which bold color blocks are separated by dark outlines, and Art Nouveau.

DEGENERATE ART

In 1937, works by Gauguin were included in an exhibition of "degenerate" art staged by the Nazis at the Haus der Kunst in Munich. This attempted to show art that fell short of the standards in art expected by the Nazis, who only cared for realistic portrayals of heroic Aryan men and women.

DID YOU KNOW?
FASCINATING FACTS ABOUT THE ARTIST AND THE TIMES IN WHICH HE WORKED

• Gauguin's guardian, Gustave Arosa, had a large art collection and some of the avant-garde artists of the day visited him there. This was where Gauguin first met the Impressionists.

• Gauguin was so inspired by Cézanne's work that he wrote to Pissarro asking him to pass on any tips from Cézanne about his techniques. Thinking that he would be flattered, Pissarro told Cézanne of this, but Cézanne was furious and from then on, hated Gauguin, believing that the younger man wanted to steal his ideas.

• For a year after he left his job at the bank, Gauguin tried to support his family as an artist in Paris. They became so poor that they had to sell many of their belongings to buy food. Then Mette insisted that they moved to Copenhagen to live with her family. Gauguin found a job there as a sales representative, but he was unsuccessful at this, too.

• After Denmark, Gauguin returned to Paris, taking his six year old son Clovis with him, but within a year, they were both undernourished and Clovis had smallpox. Eventually Gauguin's sister Maria stepped in, providing the funds to send Clovis to boarding school—and none of his children ever stayed with their father again.

• Gauguin was influenced by many different things, including Japanese prints, folk and medieval art, stained glass windows, Impressionism, Egyptian art, Cambodian sculpture, and Central and South American art. He was one of the first artists to take an interest in primitive cultures.

• Pissarro taught Gauguin about painting, but he did not understand when Gauguin became interested in expressing strong emotions and believed his ideas were old-fashioned.

• The Palace of Fine Arts at the 1889 Exposition Universelle proudly displayed the best of French art, but Gauguin's work was not included, so he organized an independent exhibition at Volpini's café.

• Gauguin loved music; he played the mandolin and once called painting "music's sister." He wanted colors and shapes in paintings to appeal to people as haunting music does—this idea was later expressed by a twentieth century Russian artist, Wassily Kandinsky.

• In 1894, some sailors made fun of Annah the Javanese. In her defense, Gauguin was involved in a brawl and he broke his ankle. While he recovered in Brittany, Annah ransacked his Parisian studio. He never saw her again.

• Despite his dreams of an idyllic life in Tahiti, Gauguin lacked the skills for this. He could neither fish nor farm as native families did, so he had to buy his food. The only food available there however, was canned or dried European produce.

- When Gauguin returned to Paris in 1893, Durand-Ruel held an exhibition of his Tahitian work. Realizing that the Parisian art world might not understand the work, Gauguin prepared his account of Tahiti for publication. He called it *Noa Noa* (meaning the Fragrant Isle) and he prepared watercolors and woodcuts to accompany it. He did not complete the work however, in time for the exhibition opening. It was only after his death that the words and pictures were published together in a book.

- Because he could not afford canvas, at first Gauguin used table linen and Mette's petticoats for painting. Later, he often painted on coarse sacking. He also spread his paint thinly to make it go further.

- Although today Gauguin is mostly known for his paintings, he was multi-talented and also created ceramics, woodcuts, wood carvings, zincographs, and written texts.

- Although he last saw his children in 1891, Gauguin thought of them every day. He pinned photographs of them on his wall in Tahiti, in order of their ages and he wrote them many letters.

- In 1901, Gauguin travelled to the Marquesas Islands, about 800 miles (1288 km) from Tahiti. He bought a piece of land from the bishop there and built a big hut from wood, palms, and bamboo.

- In 1903, Gauguin was sentenced to three months' imprisonment because he wrote articles in a local newspaper, criticizing the government about how Tahiti was being spoilt. He never served his sentence as he died while waiting for an appeal. He was fifty-four years old.

SUMMARY TIMELINE OF
THE ARTIST & HIS CONTEMPORARIES

THE LIFE OF GAUGUIN

~1848~

In the year that Gauguin is born, the Second French Revolution occurs; the California Gold Rush begins

~1855~

The first Exhibition Universelle is held in Paris, displaying French technological and economic progress; twenty-five year old Pissarro arrives in Paris from the West Indies and seven year old Gauguin arrives there from Lima

~1865~

Gauguin enters the merchant navy as an apprentice and makes his first trip on the *Luzitano* from Le Havre to Rio de Janeiro; in the USA, Abraham Lincoln is assassinated, the American Civil War ends and slavery is abolished

~1867~

In the year of Gauguin's

mother's death, another Exposition Universelle is held in Paris, with Japan participating after not trading with the West for about 200 years, triggering a craze for Japanese art and design

~1871~

Gauguin leaves the merchant navy at the end of the Franco-Prussian War and starts working as a stockbroker; he meets and begins a close friendship with the painter Émile Schuffenecker and he meets his future wife, Mette-Sophie Gad; Baron Haussmann begins modernizing Paris, knocking down slums and building long, wide boulevards

~1874~

After visiting the first Impressionist exhibition, Gauguin takes up painting; child labor is banned in France

~1879~

In the year of the fourth Impressionist exhibition, Gauguin starts collecting Impressionist paintings; he is invited to participate, but fails to submit his entries in time to be included in the catalog; Thomas Edison demonstrates the electric light bulb

~1880~

Gauguin participates in the fifth Impressionist exhibition, with six paintings and one highly finished marble bust of Mette, sculpted in 1877; the German painters Ernst Ludwig Kirchner and Franz Marc and the American sculptor Jacob Epstein are born

~1881~

Gauguin exhibits a woodcarving and eight canvases at the sixth Impressionist exhibition; Picasso is born

~1882~

At the seventh Impressionist exhibition, Gauguin exhibits twelve oil paintings and pastels and a bust of his son Clovis; Georges Braque is born

~1884~

Seurat paints *Sunday Afternoon on the Island of La Grande Jatte*

~1886~
Poverty-stricken, Gauguin works as a billposter at five francs an hour as his son is ill; he exhibits the eighth and final Impressionist exhibition; he meets Vincent and Theo van Gogh; Theo exhibits and buys some of his works; the artists Diego Rivera and Oskar Kokoschka are born

~1887~
Gauguin goes to Panama with his brother-in-law, Charles Laval and then to the island of Martinique, but suffering with dysentery and malaria, he returns to Paris; he moves in with Émile Schuffenecker

~1888~
Returning to Pont-Aven, Gauguin paints *The Vision after the Sermon*; van Gogh paints *The Yellow House at Arles* and at the end of October, Gauguin joins him in Arles, but leaves two months later

~1889~
The Eiffel Tower marks the Paris Exposition Universelle, held to celebrate the 100th anniversary of the French

Revolution; not included in the official Centennial Exhibition of French Art, Gauguin organizes an independent exhibition, described as "Paintings of the Impressionist and Synthetist Group" and now recognized as the first Symbolist exhibition

~1890~
Cézanne paints *Still life with a Basket (Kitchen Table)*; van Gogh dies

~1891~
Seurat and Theo van Gogh die; Gauguin auctions thirty of his paintings at the Hôtel Drouot in Paris, all but one are sold and he uses the money to move to Tahiti

~1893~
While Gauguin recovers from illness in Paris, Durand-Ruel holds an exhibition of his Tahitian artwork—the exhibition has a mixed reaction

~1895~
Before returning to Tahiti, Gauguin once again auctions his work at the Hôtel Drouot,

but this time the sale is not good; back in Tahiti, his health begins to fail; the Lumière brothers film the first motion pictures

~1897~
For the first time, female art students are allowed to attend the École des Beaux-Arts, the official art school in Paris; back in Tahiti, Gauguin paints *Where do we come from? What are we? Where are we going?*

~1899~
To try to make ends meet, Gauguin takes a desk job at the Office of Public Works and Surveys in Papeete, where he is living; Alfred Sisley dies

~1901~
Gauguin leaves for the Marquesas Islands and once there, his palette becomes even brighter; Queen Victoria and Toulouse-Lautrec die

~1903~
In the year of Gauguin's death, Pissarro also dies

WHAT DID HE SAY?

Here are some of the things that Gauguin said:

• "I shut my eyes in order to see"

• "Art has increasingly become the concern
of the artist and the bafflement of the public"

• "I want to suggest an exuberant and wild nature and
a tropical sun which sets on fire everything around it"

• "I am leaving to be at peace, to rid myself of the influence
of civilization. I only want to create art that is simple,
very simple. To do that I need to renew myself in
unspoiled nature"

• "Art is either plagiarism or revolution"

• "A hint—don't paint too much direct from nature.
Art is an abstraction! Study nature then brood on
it and treasure the creation which will result"

• "Look for harmony and not contrast, for what accords,
not what clashes…go from dark to light, from light to
dark…avoid motion in a pose. Each of your figures
ought to be in a static position"

• "The flat sound of my wooden clogs on the
cobblestones, deep, hollow, and powerful,
is the note I seek in my painting"

• "In painting as in music, one should look
for suggestions rather than description"

• "You will always find nourishment in the primitive arts"

• "Art has increasingly become the concern
of the artist and the bafflement of the public"

• "There is always a heavy demand for fresh mediocrity.
In every generation the least cultivated taste has
the largest appetite"

• "We never really know what stupidity is until
we have experimented on ourselves"

A WORK IN CLOSE-UP

Gauguin often described Tahiti as a tropical paradise and this is one of his dream-like visions of the place with exaggerated colors and curved lines. In Polynesia, white is associated with death and worship of the gods and this white horse drinking quietly near two other horses with riders is believed to be depicting the spiritual harmony of nature in Tahiti. The picture was painted for a local pharmacist, but he refused it as he said the horse was too green.

Twisting blue branches of the Tahitian Purao tree cut diagonally across the picture, softening the corner.

Thin paint applied in flat areas was different from the Impressionists' small patches of paint and from van Gogh's thick, swirling marks.

Real and imaginary plants and flowers give viewers the impression of abundant lush foliage.

The white horse, bending to drink, is painted with various shades of green, indicating the reflections of the surrounding vegetation. Horses were quite rare in Tahiti, but Gauguin made them part of the tranquil, mystical landscape.

The dark blue stream with orange and pink reflections flows vertically through the composition, creating a rhythmic pattern of colors and shapes.

The White Horse, 1898,
oil on canvas, 56 x 36 in/141 x 91 cm,
Musée d'Orsay, Paris, France

The red horse is painted with two shades of red: vermilion and red earth, which contrasts with the bright green grass next to it.

Just glimpsed through the tree, another horse and rider blends with the background and balances the composition.

WHERE TO SEE THIS ARTIST'S WORKS IN THE USA

There are plenty of places in the USA where you can see works by Gauguin, but it's a good idea to check with the museum or gallery before you visit in case the work you wish to see is not on display.

The Art Institute of Chicago,
Chicago, Illinois
(www.artic.edu)

The Detroit Institute of Arts,
Michigan, Illinois
(www.dia.org)

Fine Arts Museum of San Francisco,
San Francisco, California
(www.famsf.org)

The Guggenheim Museum,
New York City, New York
(www.guggenheim.org)

J. Paul Getty Museum,
Los Angeles, California
(www.getty.edu)

The Metropolitan Museum,
New York City, New York
(www.metmuseum.org)

The Museum of Fine Arts,
Houston, Texas
(www.mfah.org)

The Museum of Fine Arts,
Boston, Massachusetts
(www.mfa.org)

The Museum of Modern Art,
New York City, New York
(www.moma.org)

National Gallery of Art,
Washington D.C.
(www.nga.gov)

The Nelson-Atkins Museum of Art,
Missouri, Illinois
(www.nelson-atkins.org)

Norton Simon Museum,
Pasadena, California
(www.nortonsimon.org)

Albright-Knox Art Gallery,
Buffalo, New York
(www.albrightknox.org)

Brooklyn Museum,
New York City, New York
(www.brooklynmuseum.org)

Chrysler Museum of Art,
Norfolk, Virginia
(www.chrysler.org)

The Cleveland Museum of Art,
Cleveland, Ohio
(www.clevelandart.org)

Harvard University Art Museums,
Cambridge, Massachusetts
(www.artmuseums. harvard.edu)

Kimbell Art Museum,
Fort Worth, Texas
(www.kimbellart.org)

Memorial Art Gallery of the University of Rochester,
New York
(magart.rochester.edu)

Minneapolis Institute of Arts,
Minneapolis, Minnesota
(www.artsmia.org)

Philadelphia Museum of Art,
Philadelphia, Pennsylvania
(www.philamuseum.org)

San Diego Museum of Art,
San Diego, California
(www.sdmart.org)

WHERE TO SEE THIS ARTIST'S
WORKS IN THE REST OF THE WORLD

You can see works of art by Gauguin in many places around the world, but particularly in Europe. It's a good idea to contact the gallery or museum before you visit, to make sure that the work you wish to see is on display.

The Fitzwilliam
Museum at the University
of Cambridge,
Cambridge, England
(www.fitzmuseum.cam.ac.uk)

The State Hermitage
Museum,
St Petersburg, Russia
(www.hermitagemuseum.org)

The Louvre,
Paris, France
(www.louvre.fr)

Musée d'Orsay,
Paris, France
(www.musee-orsay.fr)

National Galleries
of Scotland,
Edinburgh, Scotland
(www.nationalgalleries.org)

National Gallery
of Canada,
Ottawa, Canada
(www.gallery.ca)

National Gallery,
London, England
(www.nationalgallery.org.uk)

Neue Pinakothek,
Munich, Germany
(www.pinakothek.de)

Art Gallery of Ontario,
Toronto, Canada
(www.ago.net)

Courtauld Institute of Art,
London, England
(www.courtauld.ac.uk)

E.G. Bührle Collection,
Zurich, Switzerland
(www.buehrle.ch)

Fondation Bemberg
Museum, Toulouse, France
(www.fondation-bemberg.fr)

Kröller-Müller Museum,
Otterlo, Netherlands
(www.kmm.nl)

Kunstmuseum Basel,
Basel, Switzerland
(www.kunstmuseumbasel.ch)

Musée de l'Orangerie,
Paris, France
(www.musee-orangerie.fr)

Musée des Beaux-Arts
de Lyon,
Lyon, France
(www.mba-lyon.fr)

Musée Gauguin,
Papeete, Tahiti
(no website)

Musée Maurice Denis,
Saint-Germain-en-Laye,
France
(www.musee-mauricedenis.fr)

Museo Nacional
de Bellas Artes, Buenos
Aires, Argentina
(www.mnba.org.ar)

Museum fur Kunst
und Gewerbe,
Hamburg, Germany
(www.mkg-hamburg.de)

The New Art Gallery,
Walsall, England
(www.thenewartgallerywalsall
.org.uk)

New Carlsberg Glyptotek,
Copenhagen, Denmark
(www.glyptoteket.dk)

The Pushkin State
Museum of Fine Arts,
Moscow, Russia
(www.museum.ru)

Royal Museums of Fine
Arts of Belgium,
Brussels, Belgium
(www.fine-arts-museum.be)

Staatsgalerie Stuttgart,
Stuttgart, Germany
(www.staatsgalerie.de)

Tate Modern,
London, England
(www.tate.org)

The Ordrupgaard
Collection,
Charlottenlund, Denmark
(www.ordrupgaard.dk)

Thyssen-Bornemisza
Museum,
Madrid, Spain
(www.museothyssen.org)

The Whitworth Art Gallery,
Manchester, England
(www.whitworth.
manchester.ac.uk)

Van Gogh Museum,
Amsterdam,
The Netherlands
(www.vangoghmuseum.nl)

Von der Heydt-Museum,
Wuppertal, Germany
(www.von-der-heydt-
museum.de)

Wallraf-Richartz-Museum,
Cologne, Germany
(www.museenkoeln.de)

FURTHER READING & WEBSITES

BOOKS

Paul Gauguin
(First Impressions),
Howard Greenfeld,
Harry N. Abrams Inc, 1993

Paul Gauguin
(Great Names),
Diane Cook,
Mason Crest Publishers,
2003

Smoking Mirror:
an Encounter with Paul
Gauguin (Art Encounters),
Douglas Rees,
Watson-Guptill Publications
Inc US, 2005

Paul Gauguin
(First Discovery),
Jean P. Chabot,
Moonlight Publishing, 2008

Paul Gauguin
(Artists in their World),
Robert Anderson,
Franklin Watts, 2003

Paul Gauguin
(Great Artists),
Adam G. Klein,
Checkerboard Books, 2006

Van Gogh and Friends
Art Book: With Cezanne,
Seurat, Gauguin, Rousseau
and Toulouse-Lautrec,
Wenda Brewster O'Reilly,
Birdcage Press LLC, 2004

Color Your Own
Gauguin Paintings,
Marty Noble,
Dover Publications
Inc, 2001

Gauguin (Getting to
Know the World's
Greatest Artists),
Mike Venezia,
Franklin Watts, 1995

Gauguin (Eyewitness Art),
Michael Howard,
Dorling Kindersley, 1992

Art on the Wall:
Post-Impressionism,
Jane Bingham,
Heinemann Library, 2009

Post-Impressionism
(Flying Start),
Pam Cutler,
Barrington Stock Ltd, 2004

Discovering Great Artists,
MaryAnn F. Kohl,
Kim Solga,
Brilliant Publications, 2003

WEBSITES

www.ibiblio.org/wm/paint/
auth/gauguin

www.paul-gauguin.net
kids.tate.org.uk/mygallery/
gallery_artist/151?page=1

www.webexhibits.org/vang
ogh/letter/18/etc-Gauguin-
GAC30.htm

www.moma.org/explore/
multimedia/audios/3/60

www.nga.gov/collection/
gallery/gg82/gg82-
main1.html

www.nationalgallery.org.uk
/artists/paul-gauguin

www.nationalgalleries.org/
collection/online_az/4:322/
result/0/4940?initial=G&
artistId=3374&artistName=
Paul Gauguin&submit=1

www.anahitadesign.com/
impressionist/gauguin.html

www.gauguingallery.com/
biography.aspx

www.artic.edu/artaccess/
AA_Impressionist/
index.html

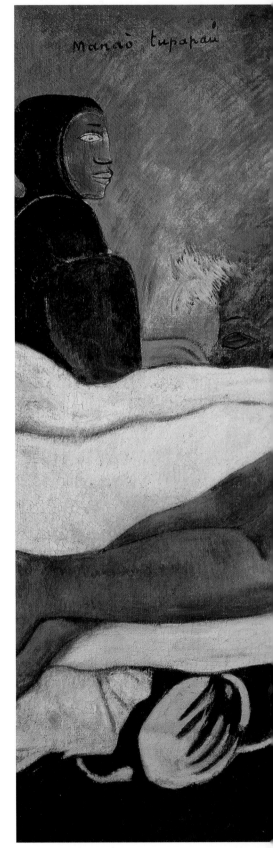

GLOSSARY

Avant-garde—A person or group at the forefront of new ideas and techniques, especially in the arts

Canvas—A heavy, closely woven fabric that artists use stretched over a wooden frame to paint on with oil paints

Cloisonnism—A movement that developed from folk art and Japanese prints and resembled a medieval enameling technique called cloisonné

Composition—Often used as a general term meaning "painting," it also means the arrangement of elements in a picture

Easter Island—An isolated volcanic island in the Pacific Ocean that had been the home of aboriginal culture for hundreds of years, but was discovered by Western explorers on Easter Sunday in 1722

Edgar Allan Poe (1809–49)—A famous American short-story writer whose story *The Raven* attracted artists' attention, as it was illustrated by Édouard Manet. Others, including Gauguin, particularly enjoyed interpreting Poe's descriptions

Nabis—The name given to a group of French artists who followed Gauguin's style of painting in flat colors. The best-known of the group were Pierre Bonnard, Édouard Vuillard, and Maurice Denis

Pigment—This usually refers to colored powder that is mixed with a liquid to make paint

Post-Impressionism—This term describes several artists who followed on from Impressionism and generally focused on personal expression, making use of color theories

Puvis de Chavannes (1824–98)—A French mural painter who worked in the fresco style, simplifying forms and emphasizing the flatness of picture surfaces, using rhythmic lines and unnatural colors to show moods. He was greatly admired by the Post-Impressionists and the Symbolists and particularly by Gauguin

Symbolism—A late nineteenth century art and literary movement which expressed ideas through symbols

Synthetism—A type of Symbolism closely associated with Cloisonnism that separated flat areas of color with black lines. It was a reaction against Impressionism using brightly colored imagery reflecting the artists' inner beliefs

Zincography—A printing process using zinc plates

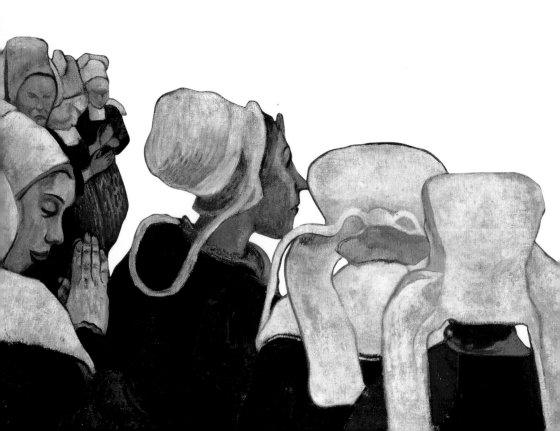

INDEX

ACKNOWLEDGMENTS

Picture Credits t=top, b=bottom, c=center, l=left, r=right, OFC=outside front cover.

Advertising Archives; 34cl. AKG (London); 8/9ct. Ann Ronan Picture Library; 15cb. Anthony Blake
Photo Library/© Rosenfeld, 14bl. Bridgeman Art Library; 10bl, 10tl, 11t, 24tl, 28br, 35br. Burstein
Collection/Corbis; OFCb. Christies Images 34/35c. Colourific!; 14/15 (background) & 14c. Fotograph Ole
Woldbye; 12t, 26tl. Gauguin Museum; 13tr, 28tl, 30tr. Giraudon; 8bl, 9bl & 9br, 10/11cb & 11br, 12c, 12b,
12/13c & 13bl, 14tl, 16tl & 16b & 16/17c, 17tr & 17br, 18tl & 18bl, 18/19cb, 19tr, 20/21t, 20cr & 20b, 22tl,
22bl, 22/23b, 23tl & 23br, 24/25t, 24/25b & 24bl, 24/25c, 26/27b, 28cl & 28/29c, 29tr & 29bl, 30/31c & 31tr,
32tr & 32/33cb, 33t. Giraudon/Bridgeman Art Library; 6tl, 8tl. Glasgow Museums; 26/27c. Mary Evans
Picture Library; 7tr. Metropolitan Museum of Art, Bequest of Sam A. Lewisohn 1951, photograph © 1993;
21bl & 21r. Museum of Fine Arts, Boston; 33br. Musée d'Orsay, Paris/Giraudon/The Bridgeman Art
Library; OFCc. National Gallery of Washington; 6cl & 6/7c & 36ct. National Maritime Museum (London);
7br. Ny Carlsberg Glyptotek, Copenhagen/The Bridgeman Art Library; OFC (main image).
Réunion des Musées Nationaux © RMN; 27r. Rudolph Staechelin Family Foundation, Basel/
The Bridgeman Art Library; OFCt. Superstock; 35tr. Telegraph Colour Library; 15tr.

NOTE TO READERS
The website addresses are correct at the time of publishing. However, due to
the ever-changing nature of the Internet, websites and content may change.
Some websites can contain links that are unsuitable for children. The publisher
is not responsible for changes in content or website addresses. We advise
that Internet searches should be supervised by an adult.